A
Southern
Woman's
Prayers

A
Southern Woman's
Prayers

Dorothy S. Warlick

Celo Valley Books
Burnsville, North Carolina

Copies of this book may be obtained by sending for each copy: $10.00 + $1.00 shipping/handling to: Dorothy Warlick, 2003 Medhurst Drive, Greensboro, NC 27410. Copies may also be ordered through the publisher.

This book was designed and produced by
Celo Book Production Service
346 Seven Mile Ridge Road
Burnsville NC 28714

ISBN 0-923687-45-9
Library of Congress Catalog Card Number 97-77166

To my treasured touchstones.
You know who you are.

— DS

Contents

Preface

I don't remember the beginning of my relationship with God. I do know it was early. I don't remember a time when I didn't talk to him.

As a young child, around four, when the wind would catch the pine branches outside my bedroom window with a soft moaning sound, I felt as if that sound was God telling me to meet him outside. I would always answer, "I'll be there in a little while." The sound would go away as if my answer was all it took to quiet it.

There wasn't much formal education in the church for my sisters and me. My grandparents attended the Methodist church every time the doors were open, but my parents' view of church was social, I'm afraid. They made sure we showed up at Christmas and Easter with a few random Sundays thrown in every now and then. Of course, we had to attend Vacation Bible School every summer. I didn't particularly care for that, except for the Kool-Aid and cookies that appeared midmorning.

Looking back, I'm increasingly aware of the influences that brought me to God and the relationship that has enriched my life. Many angels unaware were there for me, leading me in the path.

I have always felt that we women hold up more than our share of the sky and that our prayers are unique to our sex. Not to say that men don't pray as earnestly, it's just that our situation stands in the need of prayer a little more. The following prayers I have titled *A Southern Woman's Prayers.* They begin at the age of twelve, when we first enter the fellowship called womanhood.

— *Dorothy S. Warlick*

Prayers

Isn't There Some Better Way to Do This, God?

Dear God,

*Sally McConnell and I were sitting out on the
curb today.*
You know what she told me,
don't you?
Her daddy is a doctor
and he should know.
*Also, she is a Catholic, and she would go to
hell*
if she ever told a lie.
I don't think I like this idea, God.
Why can't you just go to the hospital
and get a baby?
She told me you have to take off your clothes
and all this other stuff
I would never do
if I wanted to have children.
Is this your idea?
Is this really the only way?
I won't ever have any children if that's
what you have to do to get them,
I'll tell you that!
I love Roy Rogers.

Do you think he's done that?
I hope not.
I couldn't go to any more of his pictures
if I thought he and Dale did
what Sally said.
I can't ask Mother about it.
This makes me feel sad.
Sally was laughing about it and said
her daddy had some pictures in books
I ought to see.
I told her, "No, thank you."
And went home.
I'm going to stay up here
in my room for a while.
Really, God.
Tell me what I'm supposed to think
about all of this.

                      Amen.

I Needed
Skates Worse

Thank you, God,
for the best Christmas ever.
We got up at 4:30 this morning
and Mama and Daddy
didn't even hear us
go down the stairs.
We practiced yesterday
remembering where
the creaky stairs were.
I got everything on my list.
But, God,
when Pop and Granny came
all they brought me was
one of those old war bonds.
Every Christmas, birthday, and Easter,
one of those old war bonds!
Wouldn't you think they would know
what a kid wants?
I need a pair of skates
a whole lot worse.

Oh, well,
maybe it's because they
are so old
they don't remember
what kids are really like.
Anyway, thanks for a
wonderful Christmas.

> *Amen.*

Why Do Girls Have to Have All the Bad Stuff?

Dear God,

*Mama sat me down today and started talking
about all that stuff we've had
in health class this week.
She gave me some stuff
to keep in my closet
and told me I'd need it
one day soon.
After what Sallie told me, I don't think
I like this any better than
that other stuff.
Mama said I would be a woman
when all this stuff starts.
I don't want to be a woman.
Why can't you let me stay what I am?
There's nothing wrong with that,
God. Do you make women have to
do all this stuff
because you're a man?*

*Is it because you don't want men
to have to put up with anything?
Sounds like it to me.
If you lived with Mrs. God,
she would tell you
this is a bad idea.
Please keep me from turning
into a woman
as long as you can.
Thank you ahead of time.*
                    Amen.

Thanks
for Nothing, God!

Well, God,
Mama was right:
This is no fun!
She got all teary-eyed
when I told her.
I just know she told Daddy.
He hid behind his paper tonight
when he got home,
and didn't have much to say.
I don't feel good.
If being a woman is such a big deal,
why do I have a stomachache?
Worst of all, I can't
go to the pool
until this is over.
There's nothing good about
the whole thing.
Do you do this to women
in Africa, too?

They don't even have drugstores over there
to buy this stuff.
That's not fair.
I think you should make boys
have to do something.
I don't want to make you mad at me,
God,
but I think this is a hateful thing
to do to us
just because we're girls.
I am not putting any money
in the collection plate Sunday.
I am taking it to the drugstore
to buy something
for me, instead.
I'm sorry, God.
I just think you don't
love me very much.
                    Amen.

Mama Should Have Said No, God

Dear God,
I really need your help.
I've told a huge lie and
I'm going to get caught
for sure.
We're at the lake for the summer
and Hugh, this boy next door,
asked me how old I am.
I told him sixteen.
You know I'm only thirteen
(but everybody says I look sixteen).
He asked me for a date tonight.
I thought Mama would say no
but she didn't.
She knows his mama, so
she thinks it's all right.
If he finds out I'm thirteen,
he'll be mad.
I'm really afraid he will want
to kiss me,
especially, if we go
to the drive-in
where all the other kids go.

I told my buddy Dickie
about it and he said
he'd show me how to kiss.
Just in case.
We practiced some this afternoon
in his daddy's car.
At least I know how
to keep my nose to one side.
Dickie thought it was funny
but then, he's older than I am
and he's always laughing at me.
God, I don't think there's anything
in the Bible about kissing, so
I really don't think
I've done anything wrong.
Have I?
Let me know if this is bad.
If something is bad it wouldn't be fun,
would it?

      Amen.

Help My Mama, God—
Something's Bad Wrong

Please, God,
> *Make Mama well.*
> *She's doing things she never done,*
> *and I'm scared.*
> *She cries all the time*
> *and her temper is so bad.*
> *She didn't used to be this way.*
> *She turns red in the face and*
> *has to fan herself all the time.*
> *Then she can act just like*
> *everything is OK.*
> *Dr. Jones asked me the other day*
> *if she was doing all these things,*
> *just like he'd been watching her.*
> *I started to ask him how he knew,*
> *but I didn't.*
> *Well, anyway, God,*
> *he gave her some green medicine to take.*
> *It's supposed to make her feel better.*
> *Yesterday, she got real bad,*
> *all nervous and shaky.*
> *Then she started crying*
> *and saying things she shouldn't say*

like "damn" and "hell"
and I'm sure I heard her say
"son-of-a-bitch"!
I went to get her medicine fast.
My sister said to give her
a teaspoonful in a glass of water,
but, God, she was worse
than I've ever seen her,
so I put four spoonfuls in the water
and gave it to her.
God, she was still asleep
in the hammock
when Daddy came home from work.
She didn't even wake up for supper.
She slept all night, God,
and till lunch today.
I thought I had killed her, God.
Thank you for letting her live.
I won't ever do it again, I promise.
She felt better this afternoon.
　　　　　　　　Amen.

What's
the Big Deal, God?

Dear God,
  I don't know what the big deal is.
  I've been sent to my room
  for the rest of the day
  for nothing!
  Why did they have to get
  so bent out of shape
  just because we went swimming
  with no clothes on?
  They think it's so funny to
  show the snapshots of all of us
  naked on those fur rugs . . .
  What's wrong with swimming that way?
  We're cousins, and
  kin don't count.
  Mama and Aunt Jeanne
  and Aunt Polly
  have thrown us into the
  same tub together
  for all our lives.

Why is it wrong, all of a sudden?
Harrietta is the only one with
breasts yet
and she kept them underwater.
Our parents must have
dirty minds.
Sam says he's staying out of this.
Why can't my folks do the same?
                    Amen.

Don't Let Anybody Touch Me Again, God

God,
   I was so scared today.
   Didn't you know I was in trouble?
   Old Kenny has worked in our yard
   since I was little.
   I've never been afraid of him before.
   I wasn't scared when
   he followed me into the basement
   this afternoon.
   But when he started touching me
   in private places,
   he wouldn't stop
   when I told him to.
   Why wouldn't you make him
   leave me alone, God?
   Only the man who loves you
   and wants to marry you
   is supposed to touch you
   that way,
   isn't he, God?
   Thank you for making
   Sam decide to hang out the wash
   in the basement
   while Kenny was there.

*He grabbed Kenny and told him
he'd kill him
if he ever laid a hand
on me again,
God. Sam got real mad at Kenny,
but worse,
I think he's mad at me, too.
He told me to go in the house
and not to tell
Mama and Daddy.
Sam has never been mad
at me before.
I don't know what I did
that was so wrong.
If I can't tell Mama, then
you're the only one
I can talk to about this.
Thank you, God,
for letting Sam find me,
even if he is mad
about something.*

Amen.

Don't Let Them Know
How Happy I Am to Leave, Lord

Dear God,

I'm really going to need your help.
Finally I'm getting to leave home
and be on my own.
I couldn't have stood it
one more day.
It's been so hard being born to
a crazy family.
Everyone else's family
is so normal.
Why did I have to live
with ones who aren't?
I don't want to hurt my family, Lord,
but it's time to leave them.
Let me find new friends
and get off on the right foot.

Help me to stay on the path.
Sam hugged me last night and said,
"Remember who you are."
What does he mean, God?
I can't be anybody but who I am.
I'm grown now.
Eighteen is old enough to
know what I'm doing, isn't it?
Stay with me, Lord, while I learn
to handle life by myself.
                              Amen.

This One's Different, God

God,
  He's not like all the others.
  He's older and
  back from Korea
  and going to college.
  Is that what makes him
  so attractive?
  I need someone who's older.
  He's not silly like the
  boys I've known before.
  He just walked right up and
  asked me to dance.
  He didn't dance with anyone else
  all night.
  I wonder if he's the one?
  I ask that about all of them,
  but this time, I looked at him
  while I was thinking it.

I guess I'll find out if
he ever calls me again.
Best of all, God, he's a
Sigma Chi—
only the best fraternity
in the world,
with the prettiest pin:
a Norman cross.
He's tall, too.
He kinda fits all the
important stuff, God.
Don't let him lose my address.
Is he the plan you have for me?
Let me know, God.
                    Amen.

I Had Forgotten
All About That, Lord! !

Dear Heavenly Father,
I've been so busy.
The wedding is only a week away
and this has been so exciting,
but today, Lord,
the best thing of all happened!
Pop took me to the bank
in his old truck
and wouldn't tell me
what we were going to do.
He took me back in a
little tiny room
full of drawers
with locks on them
and opened the one
that was his.
He handed me a stack
of folded papers
and smiled at me so big.
I had forgotten.
All those war bonds were there
from when I was just a baby.

Every year I remember
getting them on holidays
and wishing they were presents
I could play with instead.
Lord,
I signed my name on the backs
of all of them.
The teller added them up
and smiled.
She gave me almost
five thousand dollars
to put into my account.
I never realized until now
what Pop and Granny have been doing for me
all these years.
One bond at a time.
Providing the foundation
for this marriage.
And I thought I needed skates!
Thank you, God, for giving me Pop.
                         Amen.

This Is Not
What I Had in Mind

Dear Lord,
I only got to wear that white dress
for three hours.
It was magic.
I was Cinderella.
He was my prince.
And now, Lord,
I'm in a strange town.
This apartment is
so drab and sparse.
At home, I had a pretty room
and carpet on the floor.
He said to me,
"Let me take you away
from all this."

Oh, God, he has—
and I may never see it again.
What have I done, God?
Tell me I haven't made
a big mistake.
Give me the courage
to do without
for a while.

Amen.

I'm Leaving As Soon As I Get Out of the Driveway

Dear God,
> I need your help.
> The argument was terrible.
> I said some hurtful things.
> I think I threw a dish.
> I know I threw a dish.
> I meant to hit him.
> Worst of all,
> it started over gravy,
> his favorite beverage.
> I'm trying to learn to fix
> all his favorite things.
> But I can't make that stuff.
> We never even had it
> at my house.
> I made some tonight
> and he didn't even try it.
> Said he thought it
> was chocolate pudding,
> and laughed.
> I should have stopped there.
> But, God, he had to bring
> his mother into it.
> How good hers was.

If only I hadn't suggested
he go find her to make it.
You know, God,
you called her to heaven
two years ago.
He yelled at me.
I said I was leaving.
I picked up my bag and sweater
and slammed out the door
as loudly as I could.
It's dark and cold out here
in the car, God.
The door locked behind me
and my keys are still
in the house.
God, I can't get out
of the driveway.
Please make him start
looking for me first.
It's cold out here.

Amen.

Whose Idea Was This, Lord?

Heavenly Father,
Everyone is so excited about this baby
except me.
I act like I'm expected to,
but I'm afraid.
What made me agree to this
in the first place?
I don't know who I am yet,
and now I'm expected
to bear this new life
and know what's
best for it.

Please guide me, Lord,
and keep me from
screwing up totally.
Watch over us both
during the coming months,
and grant me a new security
and calm
to serve me in this venture
I'm not sure I'm ready
to take on.
Teach me who I am
somewhere in the process.
                    Amen.

Help Me Remember, So I Don't Do This Again

Dear God,
Just where were you
in that delivery room?
I needed you
to take away the pain.
Her daddy was the last man
I wanted to see in there,
telling me how great
I was doing.
As if I had any control
over the matter!
Why don't you give them
the experience
of pulling their upper lip
up over their head
while we stand over them
telling them
how great they're doing?

God, I don't mean
to be ungrateful.
Really, I don't.
She is so beautiful.
Thank you for her perfectness.
And most of all, God,
thank you for giving her
the ears from my side
of the family
and not his.
You are a merciful God.
                    Amen.

What Makes Him Think Diapers Weren't a Part of Fatherhood?

Heavenly Father,
A hand grenade must have
gone off in my body.
I thought the pain stopped
once the baby was here.
That apple Eve ate
didn't warrant all this.
I haven't slept for days.
I can't sit in a chair.
I'm tired of sitz baths
and breast pumps,
while her daddy prances around
like a gazelle
on the Serengeti.
And me like a water buffalo.
God, all I asked him to do was
change one little messy diaper.
His eyes glazed over
like a possum in the headlights.

"Oh, no," he said,
and disappeared from view.
Why does he get to choose the
parts of parenthood
he'll participate in?
I can't.
Would it upset the universe
if you postponed their circumcision
until the day
the firstborn comes home?
It would at least give
the new mother
some sense of justice.
Or do you not allow it
because you know it
would be vengeance?
                              Amen.

Rest in Peace, Lumbertine

Dear Father,
She has to die tomorrow.
You know how much we hate to kill her.
She's been "with me" two years
but now she has to go.
It was just so hard to get any money
from our husbands,
so my friend and I hit on the idea
of a maid every Wednesday
to spruce up the house
and put a shine on everything.
She only "charged" ten dollars a day
and the men had one day they knew
a clean house waited for them.
They didn't mind the money for that.
And now we have to lose her
before we get caught.
You know, Lord,
that we've been "Lumbertine" all this time.

It was easy at first,
playing the game,
but now the questions are getting
too close for comfort.
We've made all the
spending money we can risk.
Forgive us our deception,
but thank you for giving us
the creativity
for the idea.
I'll miss Lumbertine, God.
Maybe after a short time
to grieve,
there will be a real Lumbertine
to help out
when I need a break.
Thank you for the two years I had her.
May she rest in peace.
                    Amen.

Try to Understand Mavis Just a Little

God,
> *The whole town is talking about Mavis.*
> *That sweet little gray-haired lady*
> *has done in a bunch of people*
> *with ant poison.*
> *She sat there all sweet-like*
> *and just fed it right to them.*
> *Everyone thought she was so kind*
> *to sit there in the hospital*
> *and spoon in*
> *those peanut butter milkshakes*
> *and banana puddings.*
> *She knew all the while*
> *she was handing them over to you*
> *with every bite.*
> *Try to understand*
> *where she was coming from.*
> *It could have been any of us women.*

We all deep down know some men
we'd like to cook for like that.
Lord, you know I've shot my husband
dozens of times—
I just never pulled the trigger.
Am I less of a sinner than she?
Was she weaker than the rest of us?
Or do you suppose
she was stronger?
Anyway, God,
understand Mavis and grant her
forgiveness and mercy.
                              Amen.

She Knows Not
What She's Done, Lord

Thank you, Lord.
The surgery is over. I was so frightened.
My surgeon is worried that I might be
*   depressed*
about losing my ability to bear more children.
Help me convince her, Lord, without
jumping up and down.
(Which would hurt right now.)
She's so young, still. She couldn't understand
*   she's thrown me*
in the briar patch.

Show me the way, Lord, to assure her
I will not feel the empty-nest syndrome.
Let me find the words to express this time in
   my life
as my rebirth of self.
Thank you, Lord, for the path to the
second half of my life.
I know the way.

               Amen.

I Never Even
Asked You, Lord

I never even asked you, Lord.
I ask for so much,
this seemed out of reach.
To finish college
with three small children
still at home.
You heard my dream unspoken
and you've provided the means
for me to go.
I never heard of my grandfather's brother,
Uncle Frank.
He died so long ago.

And now, because of him,
I can finish school.
Someone I never knew
has paved the way.
Your plans for me
are part of this.
Keep that knowledge before me
as I begin
this path ahead.

                      Amen.

Socks on
a Rooster, Lord

I felt so out of place today,
back on that campus.
All those kids—
and me their mothers' age.
This is blind faith, Lord.
Keep me from running
the other way.
The degree is two full years away.
Give me the fortitude
to hang in there.
My husband says
he doesn't mind
as long as I can still
manage the children
and run the house.

I'll work with the children,
but something tells me
the house will suffer.
Will it be deceitful
to put forty-watt bulbs
in all the lights
until I have time again
for dusting?
I can cope with the dust
as long as no one
writes in it.

Amen.

Forgive Me
Ahead of Time, Lord

*All I wanted to do
was teach these children
with learning problems.
You made it all possible
for me to do.
Why now, after
showing me the plans
you had for my life,
would you send me
these terrorists?
They have no
redeeming qualities.
Their only problem is
they survived birth.
Must I lower myself
to their level?*

I have terrible plans
for tomorrow.
I am older
and I know
old age and treachery
will always overcome
youth and skill.
Forgive me for saving my hide
by breaking some rules.
                    Amen.

Have I Made
a Difference to Them?

Another year begins.
Another group of kids
with three strikes
already against them.
How can I serve so many
and make a difference?
Jakki cannot see.
That beautiful Chantelle
can only hear
my fingers speak to her.
Paul tells me about
his Down's syndrome
as if it were a cold.
Kathy complains her feet hurt.
I try to be gentle
when I tell her
her shoes are on the wrong feet.
I know so many wonderful things

I can never share with them, God.
Please tell me how to stop
taking them home with me
in my heart every day.
Please show me I'm touching
their lives, somehow.
And help me tell
that wonderful simple boy
that he can't call me
Hot Lips in class.

Amen.

Where Did You Go, Mama?

I've known for a long time
things were not the same.
Mama is disappearing so fast.
Sometimes she doesn't know me.
I know this is a disease.
She wrote plays,
and poetry, and books.
She was witty and intelligent
and beautiful.
Did you have to take
all that away?
Forgive me, God,
but I'd rather have lost her
in one terrible blow
than to see her die twice.
Forgive me for laughing
when it gets so bad.

I laugh to keep from crying.
There she stands, God,
at the top of the stairs.
She has on a pair of Nikes,
her beautiful mink hat,
and long white underwear
with little blue flowers,
and her bra over her shoulder
like a purse.
She is waving goodbye.
Please don't let this
be the last time I see her alive.
                    Amen.

I Couldn't
Be There for Her

All I did was sneak off to the beach
for a weekend.
I needed a break so badly—
my daughter's baby was due
and she couldn't travel.
So I went to her
just for two days.
No one in the family
knew how to reach me
when Mama died,
until the morning of the funeral.
I didn't stop for anything.
Sand still clinging to my jeans,
sweatshirt over a blouse,
tennis shoes . . .
I drove so hard
the whole six hours
in the cold gray rain.
Twenty miles from home

I knew I wouldn't make it on time.
The Christmas music was
so thrilling.
I told you, God,
that the very next song
would be my own private funeral
with my mother.
I waited for the pause to end
on the radio.
Thank you for guiding the
disc jockey's selection to
"Rudolph, the Red Nosed Reindeer."
I found out that you can cry
and laugh at the same time.
Mama would have loved it.
Thank you.
That song will never
mean the same again.

Amen.

Why Did You Send Him Home to Me, Lord?

Thank you for seeing me through so many
years of
this marriage.
Thank you for giving me the strength to stay.
When so many times I looked up the number
for
the bus station, but didn't call it.
Thank you for the wisdom that has come with
the years.
But, Lord, this new cross I don't think I can
carry.

Its name is RETIREMENT!
I've endured the better or worse,
but I did not marry him for lunch.
I'm being stalked.
He's rearranged the spice cabinet
in alphabetical order!
What made him think allspice and anise
needed to be the first things in front?
God, I'm starting to wonder if the bus station
is still on Elm Street.
As Greta Garbo said, Lord, I vant to be alone.
Amen.

Give Me Strength to Laugh at This, Lord

I guess I should be angry, God.
This woman who is doing everything but tap
*   dancing to get*
my husband's attention.
There he sits, grinning like a monkey, just
*   eating it up.*
Old fool! Thinks he looks so cute.
God, it wouldn't alter the universe if you
*   created in him*
one of those famous belches he brings up at
*   home right now,*
would it?
Let sweet young thing here have a vision of his
*   bathroom counter*
with nose-hair trimmer, Preparation H, Prozac,
*   and heart pills.*
She'd last one afternoon.

Put her out of her misery for sure.
Look at that, God.
She's laughing at that dumb joke of his.
She's even got her hand on his arm.
Wait till she's heard it five hundred times like I
*   have—*
she would have to move her hand fast to get
*   her fingers in her ears.*
Teach me patience, God.
My wisdom has come at such a price!
*   Amen.*

How Many Commandments Can I Break and Still Go to Heaven?

Dear Heavenly Father,
You know me well by now.
After all, we talk every day.
I've always tried to do
everything you've told me.
I've raised three children
and none of them are in prison.
I never kicked the dog,
though you know he needed it frequently.
I've been the virtuous woman
longer than anybody.
But, Lord, being good
can really get you down at my age.
I look in the mirror
and I don't know this old lady
staring back at me.
I'm getting older and want to do
things I've never done
before it's too late.
I've missed some boats, God.

Can't you put a statute of limitations
on those commandments?
There are a couple I'd really
like to eliminate
if they won't keep me out of heaven.
They're not really biggies, Lord.
I don't want to kill anyone
or bear false witness.
I'd never put any God before you.
I have everything I want,
so I'm not going to steal.
I don't covet my neighbor's ass.
(Those are your words, Lord, not mine.)
I just need to be
a little wicked for a while
so I'll have some memories
when it's time to go
to the nursing home.
Something to make them wonder
what the old woman
is smiling about.
> *Amen.*

Answers

Dear Lord,
How many women like me
are sitting in the dark
on the front porch
at two o'clock in the morning,
wondering what happened?
One by one
I cleared the hurdles
life set before me:
marriage,
raising those children,
that grinding career.
I've cleared the finish line.
I saw it ahead of me,
beckoning with open arms,
gold medal extended.
I felt so smug
and wise
and free.
My face ached
from smiling

until I stopped
to look
in a mirror
and take stock.
Who is that old woman
looking back at me?
Where did she come from?
When did all the hair
on my legs
move to my upper lip?
When did I begin to know
so many doctors
by their first names?
When did a hundred-mile drive
to the mountains
begin requiring
six pit stops?

God, this isn't fun.
I thought I'd have
some time to revel
in wisdom and maturity
before I needed
a medical road crew
to keep me operational.
This isn't funny.
But then, again,
it is
sometimes.
You've given me
opportunities
that never crossed
my mind
before.

I hear myself saying things
I'd never have dreamed of saying
when I was younger,
trying to fit
some mold everyone
told me I must.
I've sifted all my friends,
until only the truest remain
to be cherished
with all my heart.
They know I love them
and I don't have to tell them—
but I do,
every way I can.

Your kindest blessing,
I guess,
comes at the time
we need it most.
As our bodies
begin to talk back
to us,
you open our hearts
to what is truly important.
Thank you
for helping me see
the answer
before I've even finished
the prayer.
I'll go in now.

I don't need to sit out here
any longer,
wondering.
You've put me in control
of what's ahead.
Thank you, God.

                Amen.

About the Author

MS. DOTTIE WARLICK grew up in Gastonia, North Carolina, during what she calls the last age of innocence, when children stayed children longer, life was simpler, and rules were rules. Left to her own devices often and given the freedom to roam her small town, she drank in experiences and developed an insight into the diversity around her, learning to appreciate the individual qualities of those she encountered along the way.

MS. WARLICK graduated from Greensboro College in Greensboro, North Carolina, and later returned to live there with her husband and three daughters. After teaching children with special needs for twenty years, she retired to follow her dream of writing.